Juan Ponce de León

Juan Ponce de León

Gail Sakurai

Franklin Watts
A Division of Scholastic Inc.
New York • Toronto • London • Auckland • Sydney
Mexico City • New Delhi • Hong Kong
Danbury, Connecticut

For Eric, Nicholas, and Cameron—
with thanks for their patience

Note to readers: Definitions for words in **bold** can be found in the Glossary at the back of this book.

Photographs ©: Archive Photos/Hulton Getty Collection: 5 top, 45; Art Resource, NY/Erich Lessing: 38; Corbis-Bettmann: 28, 40 (Tony Arruza), 34, 35 (Jeremy Homer), 2 (Dave G. Houser), 20 (Wolfgang Kaehler), 23 (Bradley Smith), 48 (Roman Soumar); Earth Scenes/Bertram G. Murray Jr.: 46; Liaison Agency, lnc./Wolfgang Kaehler: 18; Mary Evans Picture Library: 15; North Wind Picture Archives: 36 (N. Carter), 8, 19, 27, 53; Photo Researchers, NY: 31 (Jacana/Claye), 22 (Scott Camazine), 32 (Ned Haines), 44 (NOAA/SPL); Stock Montage, Inc.: 25; Superstock, Inc.: 5 bottom, 42 (The Cummer Museum of Art and Gardens, Jacksonville), 6, 17, 50 (Stock Montage), 12; The Art Archive: 33 (Joseph Martin/Album), 10, 11 (Joseph Martin/Album/Cabildo Cathedral Burgos).

Cover illustration by Stephen Marchesi.
Map by XNR Productions, Inc.

The illustration on the cover shows Juan Ponce de León in Florida. The photograph opposite the title page shows a statue of Juan Ponce de León in San Juan, Puerto Rico.

Library of Congress Cataloging-in-Publication Data

Sakurai, Gail.
    Juan Ponce de León / Gail Sakurai.
        p. cm. — (Watts Library)
    Includes bibliographical references and index.
    ISBN 0-531-11964-5 (lib. bdg.)   0-531-16579-5 (pbk.)
        1. Ponce de León, Juan, 1460?–1521—Juvenile literature. 2. Explorers—America—Biography—Juvenile literature. 3. Explorers—Spain—Biography—Juvenile literature. 4. America—Discovery and exploration—Spanish—Juvenile literature. [1. Ponce de León, Juan, 1460?–1521. 2. Explorers. 3. America—Discovery and exploration—Spanish.] I. Title. II. Series.
E125.P7 S25 2001
975.9'01'092—dc21
                                                                                                00-051352

Contents

Christopher Columbus sailed west across the Atlantic Ocean aboard the Santa María.

Chapter One

The Early Years

When Christopher Columbus sailed across the Atlantic Ocean in 1492, he was looking for a sea route to Asia. Instead, he found a vast, wild land, previously unknown to Europeans. His discovery of what is now known as the Americas opened the gateway for a great age of exploration. Hundreds of adventurers and fortune hunters swarmed to explore and **exploit** this new land. Juan Ponce de León was one of those explorers.

Coats of Arms

Knights often painted a set of colorful symbols, called a coat of arms, on their shields. The coat of arms identified the knight's family and indicated his status.

Education and Military Training

Little is known for certain about Ponce de León's early life. He was probably born around 1460 in the town of Santervás de Campos, in the Spanish kingdom of León. He came from a **noble** family, but he was most likely a younger son who would not inherit any wealth or property. In those days, younger sons often became priests or knights. Ponce de León decided to become a knight.

One of the duties of a page was to help a knight with his armor.

One of the most famous Spanish knights was El Cid. His name comes from the Arabic *El Sayyid,* meaning "the lord." El Cid's birth name was Rodrigo Díaz de Vivar. He was a brave knight who cap-tured Valencia from the **Moors** in 1094. His deeds are celebrated in *The Song of the Cid,* a long poem composed in the twelfth century. It is one of the oldest Spanish writings still in existence.

Noble families usually sent their sons to another household for training as soldiers or knights. Instruction began around the age of seven. While Ponce de León was still a young boy, he was sent to the home of Pedro Núñez de Guzmán, an important Spanish nobleman.

During the first stage of his education, Ponce de León served as a page to Núñez de Guzmán. The duties of a page included taking care of his master's clothing, helping him to dress, and serving his food. In exchange for these services, Ponce de León was taught to read and write, ride a horse, hunt, and fight with a sword.

When he was about fourteen or fifteen, Ponce de León became Núñez de Guzmán's squire. A squire had the important responsibilities of cleaning and caring for his master's armor and weapons, and fighting beside him in battle. This was good practice for the day when he would become a knight.

Fighting the Moors

As a knight during the late 1480s, Ponce de León joined the military campaign to drive the Moors out of Spain. The

The Spanish captured Granada from the Moors in 1492.

Moors were an Arabic-speaking people from northern Africa who practiced **Islam**, a major world religion. The Moors had invaded Spain in A.D. 711. By A.D. 718, they had conquered all of Spain, except for the narrow mountainous region across the north.

The Spanish people fought back. The war against the Moors continued for several hundred years. The Spanish

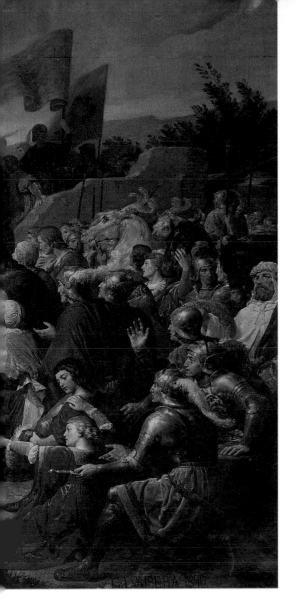

gradually regained control over one **province** after another. In the 1480s, the province of Granada in the far south was the last Moorish stronghold in Spain. King Ferdinand and Queen Isabella, the Spanish rulers, were determined to defeat the Moors. They wanted to unite all of Spain under one rule. They finally achieved their goal in January 1492, when their armies captured Granada and drove the last of the Moors from Spain. Juan Ponce de León was one of the victorious Spanish knights at that final battle.

The Alhambra

The Alhambra, a palace and fortress in Granada, Spain, was built by the Moors between 1248 and 1354. The Alhambra is famous as an outstanding example of Moorish architecture.

In Ponce de León's day, spices were native to Asia. Today, many countries across the world grow spices.

Chapter Two

Sailing With Columbus

While Ponce de León and the other Spanish knights were busy fighting the Moors, the rest of Europe was looking for new trade routes to Asia. Europeans wanted jewels, silks, and spices from eastern Asia. Sugar, coffee, tea, pepper, and spices such as nutmeg, cinnamon, and cloves were highly prized in Europe. Spices came from the Moluccas Islands, located halfway between the Philippines and Australia. People also called these islands the Indies or the Spice Islands.

The Spice Trade

Goods from Asia were brought to Europe through long and complicated trade routes. The main overland route passed through the city of Constantinople. When the **Ottoman** Empire captured Constantinople in 1453, they closed off all trade with Europe. Only the sea route through the Mediterranean remained open. The Italian cities of Genoa and Venice, which controlled all trade passing through the Mediterranean, grew rich from trade with Asia. Other European nations wanted a share of that wealth.

Christopher Columbus, a sea captain from Genoa, Italy, believed that Asia could be reached by sailing west across the Atlantic Ocean. Columbus appealed to King Ferdinand and Queen Isabella of Spain to sponsor his voyage. When the long and costly fight against the Moors ended, the Spanish rulers were free to turn their attention to other matters. Successful trade with Asia would help rebuild their wealth and power. King Ferdinand did not want to finance Columbus, but Queen Isabella agreed to provide the funds for the important voyage of discovery.

A Sea Route to Asia

In 1415, Portugal starting sending ships down the coast of Africa in hopes of finding a sea passage to eastern Asia. In 1498, Portuguese sea captain Vasco da Gama sailed around the tip of Africa and across the Indian Ocean to Calcutta, India. At last, Europeans had their long-desired sea route to the riches of Asia.

King Ferdinand and Queen Isabella of Spain

Columbus's Triumph

Christopher Columbus sailed from Spain on August 3, 1492, with three ships and ninety people. He returned to Spain seven months later with the astounding news that he had reached Asia. As proof, he brought back samples of gold, exotic tropical plants, and colorful parrots in wicker cages. He also brought six people, whom he called Indians because he believed that they were from the Indies. The six natives dressed in feathers and spoke an unusual language.

King Ferdinand and Queen Isabella welcomed Columbus and hailed him as a hero. Columbus's achievement was a huge

Conquistadors

Spaniards who explored and conquered the Americas during the late 1400s and 1500s were called **conquistadors**. In Spanish, conquistador means "a person who conquers or captures."

triumph for Spain. The news of his discovery spread rapidly throughout Europe and generated a great deal of excitement. No doubt Ponce de León was excited and inspired when he heard about it.

The Spanish rulers were anxious to establish a **colony** in this new land. They quickly made plans to send Columbus back to what they thought were the Indies. Columbus had encountered much difficulty in recruiting enough sailors for his first voyage. In contrast, there were hundreds of volunteers willing to sail with him on the second trip. Many of them were former Spanish soldiers and knights, like Ponce de León, who had fought against the Moors. These Spaniards were eager for new adventures, glory, and riches.

The Great Expedition

Christopher Columbus left Cadiz, Spain, on September 25, 1493, for his second voyage across the Atlantic Ocean. He sailed with a fleet of seventeen ships and fifteen hundred people, including a former Spanish knight named Juan Ponce de León. The party also included sailors, mapmakers, farmers, artisans, and priests. They were under orders to build a settlement, mine for gold, and convert the natives to Christianity. They brought along building and mining tools, farming equipment, and a variety of plants. Horses, cattle, chickens, sheep, and pigs were on board too.

The fleet stopped at the Canary Islands, off the northwest coast of Africa, to restock their supplies of food and fresh-

water. They left the Canaries on October 12, 1493. With fine weather and calm seas, they arrived in the Caribbean Sea just three weeks later. It must have been a great thrill for Ponce de León to be one of the first Europeans to see this land.

Landing at a previously unexplored island, Columbus claimed it for Spain and named it Dominica. Sailing on, the **expedition** came across a number of small islands. At every new island they encountered, Columbus claimed the land for Spain and gave it a Spanish name. A few years later, when Ponce de León went exploring on his own, he would follow the example of Columbus. Ponce de León would claim all of his discoveries for Spain and give the lands Spanish names.

After a long journey across the Atlantic Ocean, Columbus and his crew were happy to see land.

Puerto Rico is a mountainous, tropical island.

Eventually, Columbus and his party sighted an island that was much larger than the others. Columbus described it as "very lovely and very fertile." They continued sailing along the island's southern coast until they reached a large bay. On November 19, 1493, Columbus dropped anchor and went ashore. He named the island San Juan Bautista and claimed it for Spain. Within a few years, this island would play an important role in Ponce de León's life. Today, San Juan Bautista is known as Puerto Rico.

Finally, the fleet sailed to Hispaniola, the island where Columbus had established a small fort called La Navidad during his first voyage in 1492. He had left forty people behind at La Navidad nearly a year before. They would surely be overjoyed to see Columbus's party, fresh food, and supplies. Columbus signaled his arrival with flares and cannons.

It seemed very strange that the people at La Navidad did not answer the signals. When Columbus and Ponce de León went ashore, they discovered the reason. The fort was in ruins, and all forty people were dead.

Hispaniola

Today the island of Hispaniola is divided into two countries. The Republic of Haiti occupies the western third of the island, while the Dominican Republic covers the eastern two-thirds of Hispaniola.

The explorers learned the full story from the Taino Indians who lived on Hispaniola. The Spaniards from La Navidad had stolen food and gold from the Indians. When the Spaniards started ransacking the Taino villages and stealing their women, the Indians struck back. The Taino people, who had been friendly and peaceful toward Columbus, had killed all the Spaniards and burned down the fort. Columbus abandoned the site at La Navidad and established his colony about 75 miles (121 kilometers) further east. He named the new settlement Isabella.

This illustration shows the massacre at La Navidad.

The island of Dominica is one of many in the Caribbean Sea that the Spaniards explored.

Chapter Three

Conquering Hispaniola

When the Spanish first arrived in the Caribbean in 1492, the islands had already been inhabited for thousands of years. The people who lived there called themselves Taino, which means noble or gentle. The Taino came to the Caribbean islands by canoe from South America. Columbus wrote that Taino canoes were "made out of the trunk of a tree, all of one piece and wonderfully worked. Some are very large, holding as many as forty-five men."

Cassava

Ponce de León grew **cassava** near his home on the eastern shore of Hispaniola. Cassava, a bushy plant with greenish-yellow flowers and long, thick roots, is native to the tropical regions of the Americas. The plant grows up to 8 feet (2 meters) high, and the roots grow up to 3 inches (8 centimeters) thick and 36 inches (91 cm) long. Cassava is a popular food in the tropics. The roots can be eaten like potatoes or ground into flour for making bread and porridge. Tapioca, a starch used in puddings, comes from cassava roots.

The Taino lived in small villages, and each village was ruled by a *cacique*, or chief. Their homes were straw huts called *bohíos*. According to Spanish priest Bartolomé de las Casas, a Taino village had "houses that were very artfully made, although of straw and wood; and there was a plaza with a road leading to the sea, very clean and straight, made like a street."

The Taino slept in swinging beds called *hamacas*, similar to present-day hammocks. Hunting, fishing, and farming were the main Taino occupations. They grew crops such as pineapple, sweet potato, corn, squash, and cassava.

In the late 1400s, the Taino's peaceful way of life was threatened by two groups of newcomers. First, the fierce, warlike Carib Indians of South America began moving into the Caribbean. The Caribs frequently attacked and raided Taino villages. Second, the arrival of the Spanish conquistadors destroyed the Taino civilization forever.

Conquering the Taino

Ponce de León was one of the soldiers who protected the Spanish settlement of Isabella on Hispaniola. His training and experience as a knight in Spain helped him excel at the new

Today, a few trees stand on the site of Isabella. It is located in what is now the Dominican Republic.

job. Isabella turned out to be a poor location for a town. It was built on marshy ground, and food rotted in the humid atmosphere. Mosquitoes plagued the colonists.

The colonists eventually abandoned Isabella and built a new town named Santo Domingo near the southern coast of Hispaniola. Santo Domingo was in a healthier location than Isabella, and it was near a gold mine. Nevertheless, the town still had problems. Many colonists fought among themselves. They refused to obey the authority of Columbus, who was in charge of the colony. Columbus was not a very good leader. He was mainly interested in exploring, and he frequently sailed off. When Columbus was away, his brothers, Bartholomew and Diego, were in charge.

Most of the Spaniards did not want to do any of the hard work involved in mining gold or raising crops. They were only interested in making a quick fortune and then returning to Spain as wealthy people. They forced the Taino to do the mining and farming for them. When the colonists discovered that there was very little gold on Hispaniola, they launched a revolt against Columbus. Ponce de León and the other soldiers loyal to Columbus had to stop the revolt and restore order.

Columbus had been ordered to send gold back to Spain, but there was not much gold on Hispaniola. In desperation, he imposed a tax of gold dust on the Taino Indians. Every male Taino over the age of fourteen was required to pay a small container of gold dust every three months. Anyone who failed to pay had his hands cut off as punishment.

In February 1495, Columbus rounded up five hundred Taino Indians and shipped them to Spain to be sold as slaves. A month later, the peaceful Taino finally rebelled against this terrible treatment and attacked the Spaniards. The Indians' stone axes were no match for the Spanish soldiers' swords and firearms. Thousands of Taino were killed, and hundreds more

Spaniards stand guard over the Taino Indians as they mine for gold.

only escaped by fleeing to the mountains or to neighboring islands. Some Taino committed suicide rather than serve the Spanish or endure further cruelties.

The Spanish had brought many diseases with them. The American Indians had no natural resistance against these European diseases, and a great many of them fell ill and died. Soon, there were not enough Taino to do all the work, so the Spanish began importing slaves from Africa to work in the mines and fields. There were about thirty thousand Taino on Hispaniola when the Spanish arrived in 1492. By 1530 there were none.

Family Matters

Unlike most of the Spanish conquistadors who came to the Americas, Ponce de León decided to settle there and make it his home. He worked hard and became known as a brave soldier and a strong fighter. He later became the captain of the armed forces on Hispaniola. By 1500, Ponce de León was a respected citizen of Santo Domingo. He was described as having a healthy reddish color and "a pleasing face." In 1502, he married a Spanish woman named Leonor. She was the daughter of an innkeeper in Santo Domingo. They had four children—three girls named Juana, María, and Isabel, and a boy named Luis.

In 1504, there was a Taino uprising in Higüey, an eastern province of Hispaniola. Nicolás de Ovando, the new governor of Hispaniola, sent Ponce de León to lead an armed force of three hundred soldiers to put down the revolt. Ponce de León thoroughly defeated the rebellious Taino Indians. As a reward, Ovando appointed him as deputy governor of Higüey. While deputy governor, Ponce de León was in charge of building two towns in Higüey. Salvaleón was on the coast, while Santa Cruz de Aycayagua was built farther inland. Ponce de León's duties included distributing land and American Indian workers to the Spanish settlers in the province.

The Spaniards often treated the American Indians cruelly.

The Taino are working to preserve their cultural and tribal practices.

Chapter Four

Governor of Puerto Rico

The Taino Indians in Higüey often traded with other Taino who lived on the neighboring island of San Juan Bautista. One day, an Indian from San Juan arrived in Higüey with a large gold nugget and tales of gold mines on the nearby island. Governor Nicolás de Ovando decided to send Ponce de León to San Juan Bautista to learn if the stories of gold were true. Ponce de León sailed to San Juan with five ships and two hundred people.

Ponce de León's expedition landed on the west coast of San Juan. A group of Taino people welcomed them. The Taino took Ponce de León and his party to meet their *cacique*, Agüeybaná. The Taino chief welcomed the group with traditional ceremonies and feasts.

Mining for Gold

Ponce de León sent members of his expedition to look for gold. With the help of the local Taino people, they gathered large samples of the precious metal. Then, Ponce de León and his party returned to Hispaniola to report to the governor on their good fortune.

In July 1508, Governor Ovando sent Ponce de León back to San Juan Bautista to establish a permanent colony there. As they did on Hispaniola, the colonists forced the Taino to work for them. They built a village and a fort and planted crops. Then they began mining for gold. Later, they created a **foundry,** or factory, for processing and refining gold.

On August 8, 1508, Ponce de León founded the town of Caparra near a large, beautiful bay on the north coast. Ponce

Borinquén

Borinquén is the Taino Indian name for the island now known as Puerto Rico. Borinquén means "land of the brave lord" in the Taino language. Puerto Ricans still frequently use the Taino word to refer to their home and themselves. For instance, Puerto Rico's national anthem is called "La Borinqueña."

de León named the bay Puerto Rico, which means "rich port" in Spanish. Gradually, people started calling the island Puerto Rico instead of San Juan Bautista.

Many explorers hoped to find gold.

Ponce de León had the Indians build him a large, sturdy house in Caparra. It was not as impressive as his stone house in Higüey. The Caparra house was made from whitewashed mud, and high walls surrounded the property.

Ponce de León grew rich from his share of the gold mines and the income from his farms on Hispaniola and Puerto Rico. As the leader of the colony, he was the most important and powerful person on Puerto Rico. In 1509, King Ferdinand of Spain officially appointed Ponce de León as the first governor of Puerto Rico.

San Juan

In 1521, Spanish colonists from Caparra founded the city of San Juan. Today, San Juan is Puerto Rico's capital and largest city, with a population of about half a million people. This photograph of Old San Juan shows *El Morro,* a large military fortress that was begun in 1539 and completed in the late 1700s.

Conquering the Taino

The Spanish colonists' relationship with the Taino on Puerto Rico followed the same pattern as on Hispaniola. The Spaniards forced the Indians to mine for gold, plant and tend crops, and build roads and houses. Before long, the Taino on Puerto Rico grew angry and rebellious. But most of them were afraid to openly oppose the Spanish because they thought that the Spaniards were gods. Gods were **immortal** and did not die. If Spaniards could be killed, it would prove that they were humans, not gods. Some of the Taino came up with a plan to try to kill a Spaniard.

The Taino waited for the right opportunity. One day, a group of Taino was guiding a Spaniard named Diego Salcedo across the island. When they came to a river, the Taino offered to carry Salcedo across on their shoulders. In the middle of the river, they dropped Salcedo and held him under the water until he stopped breathing. Then they watched the body for three days. They wanted to be absolutely certain that he was dead.

Finally convinced that the Spaniards were not gods, the Taino rebelled and attacked the Spanish colonists in 1511. Ponce de León personally took command of the Spanish forces, and the rebellion was quickly put down. Although the Taino had thousands of people and the Spaniards had only a few hundred soldiers, the Indians' main weapons were stone axes. The Spanish had swords, crossbows, guns, and cannons. Thousands of Taino were killed, including

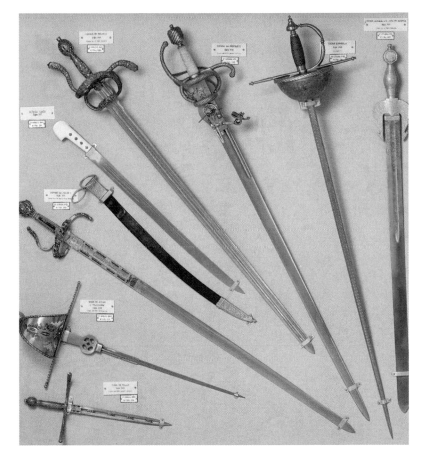

These Spanish swords are from the 1500s and 1600s.

33

their chief, Agüeybaná. Many Taino fled to the mountains or to neighboring islands, and some committed suicide.

There were nearly fifty thousand Taino on Puerto Rico in 1493, when the first Spanish explorers arrived. As had happened on Hispaniola, large numbers of American Indians died from European diseases. Within fifty years, Spanish cruelty and diseases had wiped out the entire Taino population of Puerto Rico.

Trouble With Diego Columbus

In 1511, the Spanish government decided that Diego Columbus, the son of Christopher Columbus, had the right to govern all the lands his father had discovered. Diego Columbus quickly removed the existing officials on Hispaniola and Puerto Rico and appointed his own friends and supporters instead. Ponce de León was no longer governor of Puerto Rico.

Not wanting to stay on Puerto Rico under Diego Columbus's rule, Ponce de León began to look about for a new adventure. He had heard stories from the Taino of a beautiful island called Bimini, located somewhere to the north of Cuba. Ponce de León decided to look for Bimini. If the king agreed to his plan, any new lands that

Ponce de León discovered would be his to govern. Diego Columbus would have no claim to them. Perhaps Ponce de León was also intrigued by tales about a magical fountain of youth that was supposed to be on Bimini.

Alcazar de Colon was built in 1509 for Diego Columbus. Now it is a museum in the Dominican Republic.

This fountain is in front of Hotel Ponce de León, which is now part of Flagler College in Saint Augustine, Florida.

Chapter Five

The Fountain of Youth

The Fountain of Youth. Those four words have conjured up a mystical, magical image in the minds of dreamers for centuries. Legends claim that the Fountain of Youth is a spring or stream whose clear, sparkling waters have the power to restore youth. Anyone who drinks from the imaginary spring would remain young forever.

Such tales were common in Europe during Ponce de León's era. The stories about Bimini that he heard from the

The Epic of Gilgamesh

The Epic of Gilgamesh, a long **Babylonian** poem, is one of the oldest and greatest works of world literature. It was written about 2000 B.C. in ancient **cuneiform** script on twelve clay tablets. This photograph shows a fragment of the work. The poem recounts the many adventures of the hero, Gilgamesh, who was king of the ancient city of Uruk, and his search for eternal life. Gilgamesh becomes afraid of death after Enkidu, his dearest friend and companion, dies. He seeks out a wise old man to learn the secret of immortality. The wise man reluctantly tells him that the plant of eternal youth grows at the bottom of the sea. Gilgamesh dives into the water and finds the plant, but when he stops to rest on the way home, a snake steals the plant from him. Grief stricken, he returns to Uruk to live out the rest of his days.

Taino Indians on Puerto Rico were remarkably similar. In fact, legends of eternal youth or eternal life are a theme common to many religions and cultures, from the myths of the ancient Greeks to modern-day novels and movies.

The Island of Bimini

We will never know for certain whether Ponce de León believed the tales about a fountain of youth. Perhaps he set out to find Bimini because he hoped to discover the legendary fountain. More likely, he was looking for gold and a rich, fertile land to colonize.

The Americas were vast and mysterious and contained many wonders that would have been unimaginable in Europe only a few short years earlier. If Columbus could accidentally stumble upon an entire new continent, then finding a mythical spring that restored lost youth did not seem so far-fetched.

The Seven Cities of Cíbola

Ponce de León was not the only conquistador to seek out an ancient legend in North America. American Indians told the Spanish explorers stories about seven rich cities in a land called Cíbola. The tales claimed that the streets of Cíbola were paved with gold, and the buildings were adorned with precious jewels. In 1540, Francisco Vásquez de Coronado led an expedition in search of the legendary Seven Cities of Cíbola. Coronado discovered six Zuni Indian villages near what is now Gallup, New Mexico. Convinced that he had found Cíbola, Coronado captured the settlements. To his great disappointment, they contained no gold or other riches. The location of Cíbola remains a mystery.

This photograph shows the west coast of North Bimini.

Chapter Six

La Florida

In February 1512, King Ferdinand of Spain gave Juan Ponce de León permission to locate and colonize Bimini. Ponce de León made preparations for a long voyage. He finally set out to find Bimini and the Fountain of Youth on March 3, 1513. Ponce de León sailed from San Germán, on the west coast of Puerto Rico. Sixty people were in the expedition, and they sailed on three ships—the *Santa María de Consolación*, the *Santiago*, and the *San Cristóbal*.

The three ships set a course northwest through the Bahamas, a chain of numerous small islands north of Cuba. Ponce

Ponce de León first explored Florida in 1513.

de León explored the Bahamas for almost a month, looking for gold and the legendary fountain. He stopped at Grand Turk Island to pick up supplies of food and water. On March 14, the expedition stopped again to rest for a few days at San Salvador, the first island discovered by Columbus in 1492.

Leaving San Salvador, the three ships sailed northwest again until they sighted land on March 27, 1513. The following day, Ponce de León went ashore and claimed the land for the king of Spain. He named the area, which he believed to be a large island, *La Florida*. Many historians believe that the name comes from *Pascua Florida*, the Spanish term for Easter, because Ponce de León was there during the Easter season.

The Gulf Stream

On April 8, 1513, the three ships headed south along the east coast of Florida, but a heavy current slowed them down. The current was pushing them back in spite of a strong, favorable wind filling their sails. Even with the anchors down, the ships were in danger of being carried north. Ponce de León had discovered the Gulf Stream, one of the world's most powerful ocean currents.

The Gulf Stream is a swift-flowing, underwater stream that originates in the western Caribbean Sea. It flows into the Gulf of Mexico and through the Straits of Florida, the narrow channel between the tip of Florida and Cuba. Then the Gulf Stream carries warm water northeast along the North American coast to the Grand Banks, off Newfoundland. There, it breaks up into several currents flowing in various directions.

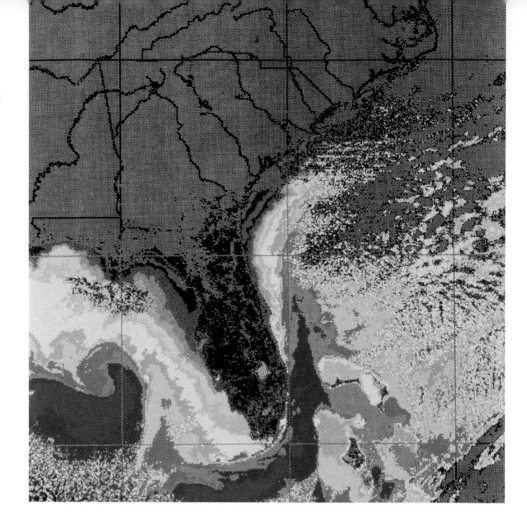

This computer image shows the Gulf Stream flowing around the southeastern United States. The Gulf Stream is the yellow area (center right) moving eastward.

By riding the Gulf Stream, ships could sail swiftly to Europe. The Gulf Stream quickly became an important trade route between the Americas and Europe.

More Discoveries

Ponce de León and his expedition continued to sail south, exploring along the Florida coast. They searched for signs of gold and the mythical fountain. After several days of travel, they spotted a village. A group of Ais Indians appeared to be signaling for the ships to land. When a party of Spaniards approached the shore in a small boat, the Indians suddenly tried to seize the boat. A fight broke out. Two of the Spanish explorers were wounded in the brief battle. A little farther south at a place Ponce de León named Santa Cruz, the

This illustration shows Ponce de León searching for the Fountain of Youth.

Dry Tortugas National Park

The Dry Tortugas are a cluster of seven small coral islands about 70 miles (113 km) west of Key West, Florida. This photograph shows Bush Key, one of the islands in the Dry Tortugas. The area is known for its abundant marine life and the hundreds of shipwrecks in the surrounding reefs and shoals. In 1992, the Dry Tortugas became a United States National Park.

Spaniards captured another Indian and forced him to act as their guide.

The three ships continued down the coast and rounded the Florida Keys, a string of small islands. Ponce de León thought that the islands' rocky profiles looked like suffering people. He called the islands *Los Martires*, or the **martyrs**.

Ponce de León thought that Florida was a large island, so he decided to try sailing around it. On May 8, 1513, he stopped at a group of small islands to supply his ships. He named the islands the Tortugas, which is the Spanish word for "turtles," because of the large number of sea turtles he found there. But he did not find any freshwater on the islands. Later, the word "dry" was added to the islands' name, to indicate that there was no source of freshwater there.

Ponce de León sailed around the southern tip of Florida and into the Gulf of Mexico. Then he made his way north along the gulf coast of Florida as far as present-day Sanibel Island. After another encounter with unfriendly American Indians, Ponce de León decided to turn around and head home to Puerto Rico.

There are several possible explanations for the hostility Ponce de León encountered from American Indians in Florida. Perhaps they simply were not as friendly as the Taino of Hispaniola and Puerto Rico. Indians who traded among the Caribbean islands may have ventured as far north as Florida and warned the natives there about the Spaniards' cruelty toward the Taino. Or the Florida Indians might have already encountered other Spaniards and learned firsthand about Spanish behavior. Spanish ships could have come to Florida looking for American Indians to capture and take to Hispaniola or Puerto Rico as slaves.

A Year of Discoveries

In 1513, the same year that Ponce de León discovered Florida, another Spanish explorer, Vasco Núñez de Balboa, crossed Central America. Balboa became the first European to see the eastern shore of the Pacific Ocean.

When Ponce de León saw the coastline of Yucatán, he thought the peninsula was an island.

Ponce de León stopped at Cuba on the way home. He also landed on the Yucatán peninsula of Mexico, which he thought was another island.

Ponce de León returned home to Puerto Rico in September 1513. He had discovered and named Florida, the Tortugas islands, and the Yucatán peninsula of Mexico. He was the first known Spanish explorer to set foot on the mainland of the North American continent. Although other Europeans, including the Vikings, may have visited there earlier than Ponce de León, no records exist of those expeditions. Ponce de León receives the official credit because he was the first to record his discoveries. However, he never did find Bimini or the Fountain of Youth.

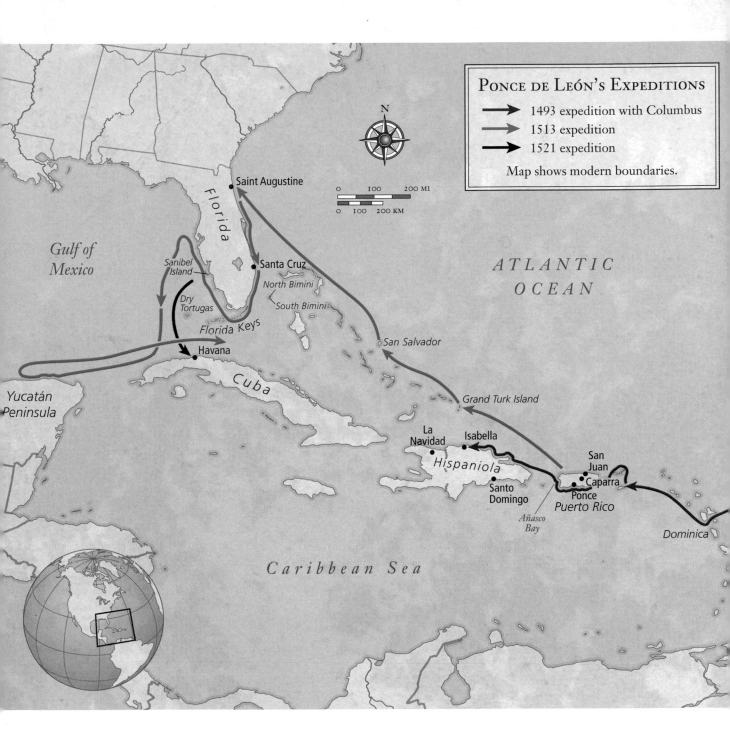

PONCE DE LEÓN'S EXPEDITIONS

→ 1493 expedition with Columbus
→ 1513 expedition
→ 1521 expedition

Map shows modern boundaries.

N

0   100   200 MI
0   100   200 KM

Gulf of
Mexico

Florida

Saint Augustine

Sanibel
Island

Dry
Tortugas

Florida Keys

Santa Cruz

North Bimini

South Bimini

San Salvador

ATLANTIC
OCEAN

Havana

Cuba

Grand Turk Island

Yucatán
Peninsula

La
Navidad   Isabella

Hispaniola

San
Juan
Caparra

Santo
Domingo   Ponce

Puerto Rico

Añasco
Bay

Dominica

Caribbean Sea

Ponce de León

Chapter Seven

Return Trip

In 1514, Ponce de León sailed to Spain to report his discoveries to the king. King Ferdinand was pleased with the news. He granted permission for Ponce de León to colonize Florida and to continue the search for Bimini.

Ponce de León returned to Puerto Rico in 1515. Before he could carry out his plans to colonize Florida, he was asked to lead an army to conquer the Carib Indians. The Caribs were fierce, aggressive fighters from nearby islands. They frequently attacked Hispaniola and Puerto Rico. Between 1515 and 1521, Ponce de León fought the Caribs.

The Final Voyage

Finally, on February 21, 1521, Ponce de León set out to colonize Florida. The expedition sailed from Puerto Rico with two ships and two hundred people, including priests, farmers, and artisans. They brought along fifty horses and farm animals such as cattle, sheep, pigs, and chickens. The expedition's supplies included food, plants and seeds, tools, farming equipment, and weapons.

The colonists landed on the west coast of Florida near Sanibel Island. They began building a settlement. One day, Ponce de León led a group into the forest to hunt for food. Suddenly, they were surrounded and attacked by Indians. The fighting was brief but fierce. Several Spaniards were killed, and Ponce de León was struck by an arrow that lodged deeply in his thigh. It was a severe wound, and there was no doctor in the small colony. The colonists carried Ponce de León to his ship. They set sail for the nearest Spanish settlement on Cuba, where he could receive proper medical attention.

In spite of medical care from a Cuban doctor, Ponce de León's wound refused to heal properly. It became dangerously infected, and he never recovered. Ponce de León died in Havana, Cuba, in July 1521.

However, Ponce de León's influence in North America lives on. He claimed Florida for Spain, and he was instrumental in the founding of Puerto Rico as a Spanish colony. Although today Florida and Puerto Rico are both part of the United States, Spanish culture and language are still very

This illustration shows Spanish soldiers carrying Ponce de León to his ship.

important there. Ponce de León's legacy is also remembered through the story of his search for the Fountain of Youth. The idea of eternal youth intrigues people in modern times as much as it did in Ponce de León's era.

In 1908, Ponce de León's remains were finally returned to Puerto Rico. He is buried in the Cathedral of San Juan Bautista, in the capital city of San Juan. The inscription on his tomb reads: "Beneath this stone repose the bones of the valiant Lion whose deeds surpassed the greatness of his name."

León

León is the Spanish word for "lion."

53

Timeline

1460	Juan Ponce de León born
1492	Spain defeats the Moors Christopher Columbus explores the Caribbean
1493	Ponce de León sails with Columbus on his second trip to the Caribbean
1508	Spanish colonists led by Ponce de León colonize Puerto Rico
1509	Ponce de León becomes governor of Puerto Rico
1513	Ponce de León explores Florida
1521	Ponce de León dies in Havana, Cuba
1565	St. Augustine, Florida, founded
1908	Ponce de León's body returned to Puerto Rico and reburied

Glossary

Babylonian—of or from ancient Babylonia and its people, culture, or language

cassava—a plant native to the Americas; its long, thick roots are a major food source in tropical regions.

colony—a territory that is far away from the country that governs it

conquistador—a Spanish person who explored and conquered the Americas

cuneiform—an ancient form of writing that uses combinations of wedge-shaped marks to form syllables and words

expedition—a journey made for a definite purpose or the group making such a journey

exploit—to make use of unfairly for one's own benefit

foundry—a building or factory where metal is melted and poured into molds

goods—items that can be bought or sold

immortal—living or lasting forever

Islam—a religion based on belief in Allah and in Muhammad as his prophet

martyr—a person who suffers greatly or dies rather than give up his or her religion or principles

Moors—people from northern Africa who speak Arabic and practice Islam

noble—of very high birth or rank

Ottoman—another name for Turkey or its people

province—a part of a country having a government of its own

To Find Out More

Books

Dolan, Sean. *Juan Ponce de León*. New York: Chelsea House, 1995.

Fritz, Jean. *Around the World in a Hundred Years: From Henry the Navigator to Magellan*. New York: G. P. Putnam's Sons, 1994.

Heinrichs, Ann. *Florida*. Danbury, CT: Children's Press, 1998.

Videos

Ponce de León: The First Conquistador. A&E Home Video, 1995.

The Quest for the Fountain of Youth. A&E Home Video, 1995.

Organizations and Online Sites

Library of Congress
101 Independence Avenue SE
Washington, DC 20540
http://www.loc.gov/
The Library of Congress maintains a website with information on American history. The online exhibition about Christopher Columbus, "1492: An Ongoing Voyage," is especially interesting.

Museum of Florida History
500 South Bronough Street
Tallahassee, FL 32399-0250
http://dhr.dos.state.fl.us/museum/
The Museum of Florida History has five locations in Tallahassee. Each site highlights a different period in Florida's past, from the Pleistocene era to the present day.

National Park Service
1849 C Street NW
Washington, DC 20240
http://www.nps.gov/
The U.S. National Park Service administers all national parks and national historic landmarks, including Dry Tortugas National Park, San Juan National Historic Site, and St. Augustine Town Plan Historic District.

A Note on Sources

When I am ready to begin research on a new project, the first thing I do is sit down in front of my computer. Computers and the Internet make life so much easier for researchers and writers. To learn some general background information on my subject, I look at two or three encyclopedias on CD-ROM. Encyclopedia articles often give me ideas for related topics to research. Some of the other subjects I read about while researching Ponce de León were Puerto Rico, Florida, Fountain of Youth, Bimini, Tortugas, Gulf Stream, Christopher Columbus, and Moors.

Next, I use my computer and the Internet to search the databases of my local libraries. Once I know what sources are available, I request the books and other materials that I think will be helpful. I always try to find as much information as I can from a variety of different sources. For instance, in addition to books on my main subject and related topics, I look for videos, articles in periodicals, and Internet websites. Also, whenever time and money allow, I like to visit the places I write about. Traveling to a location can help give writers a better feel for the subject.

I try to use primary sources whenever possible. Unfortunately, while researching Ponce de León, I discovered that no original materials were available. Unlike other explorers such as Columbus, none of Ponce de León's letters, journals, or other written documents still exist. I had to rely upon secondhand accounts in piecing together the story of Ponce de León's explorations and discoveries. I found Sean Dolan's *Juan Ponce de León* and *Discovers of the New World* by Josef Berger especially useful.

I really enjoy doing research—it makes me feel like a detective who is solving a mystery. I think it is fun to track down all the leads and discover "the truth." I always learn many new things that I never even imagined before I started. By the time I have collected all the available information, I have a good idea of how to approach the subject. I also have a working outline for the book in my head. Then comes the most difficult part—the actual writing and revising. I hope you think the result is worth all the hard work.

—*Gail Sakurai*

Index

Numbers in *italics* indicate illustrations.

About the Author

Gail Sakurai is the author of numerous nonfiction books for young readers. She specializes in writing biographies of famous people and books about American history. She has written biographies about living people and historical figures: *Mae Jemison: Space Scientist*, *Stephen Hawking: Understanding the Universe*, and *Paul Revere*. Her American history books include *The Liberty Bell*, *The Jamestown Colony*, *Asian-Americans in the Old West*, and *The Thirteen Colonies*. She is a member of the Society of Children's Book Writers and Illustrators. Ms. Sakurai lives in Cincinnati, Ohio, with her husband and two sons. When she is not researching or writing, she enjoys traveling with her family and visiting America's historical sites.